Following a prologue that introduces the author, this book is chock full of practical and ethereal ('heavenly') advice on Christian meditation, based on years of personal experience and teaching the practice to others. After the author's 12 steps to personal meditation, the reader will be wise to 'read & reflect' on passages the rest of the way through Teresa Yerkes' latest of three books. Why? Because it'd be a travesty to miss gems like this: "If I want to walk in the Spirit, I need to spend time where the Spirit is - in the center of my being." If you've never practiced Christian meditation, 'Come Closer' is a good; no, a very good place to start! -George Allen

"Come Closer" is an excellent book on its own merit but is also a wonderful addition to Teresa Yerkes' book series on Christian Meditation. "Come Closer" guides you through what gifts we can expect through regular meditation with God and reminds you of the patience and grace you will be given on the journey. -Jennifer Kurman

I just completed Come Closer by Teresa Yerkes. I thoroughly enjoyed the book and the advice therein, but I believe what I appreciate most about the book is the Author's reassurance to those growing in Christian meditation that a lifestyle of

meditation is a practice that takes time and our journeys are different, yet, similar enough for GOD to create beautiful experiences like this book. -Odessa Patton

You will laugh and cry as you take this incredibly personal journey with Teresa. She never judges but asks the reader questions that really make you stop and think about your relationship with God. -Vicki Simek

If you are looking for a clear and concise way to meditate, "Come Closer" is the book for you. Teresa takes you on her journey of discovering how she reached the best process of how meditation worked for her and how it will work for you. She teaches you step by step how to achieve the perfect state of mind to meditate. It is book that is easy to read and worth keeping on your desk or nightstand for continued reference as it is that good! This is a book you will love and cherish. -Carole Williams

Dedicated to those who desire a closer walk with our Lord.

CONTENTS

PROLOGUE

"Martha, Martha," the Lord answered, "you are worried and upset about many things, but few things are needed—or indeed only one. Mary has chosen what is better, and it will not be taken away from her.""[1]

I am a doer and an efficient doer at that. The thought of just sitting with God with no agenda didn't seem like a responsible activity when there was so much to do. At the time as a type A personality, I was working as an organizational development manager in a large corporation. I also had other roles, as wife, mother of three teenagers, supporting my husband's business, church activities, and community responsibilities. When I recall my initial experience with Christian meditation, settling into a regular practice wasn't a walk in the park. I remember days when I couldn't stand the thought of just sitting and resting in the presence of God.

We live in a rural area in a Victorian style rancher. During the week, I'd come home from work, and the first thing I wanted to do was change out of my suit into something more comfortable. I'd come into the house and head for the bedroom. Now dressed in blue jeans and a t-shirt, I was ready to take on whatever was next. Heading down the hallway, I'd stop by my sitting room, look around and wonder if I had time to meditate. The room is in the center of our house. It is a small room, furnished with a chaise lounge chair, a recliner, kneeling chair, and an ornate media cabinet. There are French doors leading out to the balcony overlooking a large yard with open space that ends with fifteen acres of woodlands behind it. I selected this room for the peaceful and quiet ambience. I love spending time reading here and my plan was to use the space for meditation as well.

Standing in the hallway, staring at my kneeling chair and the inviting peaceful space, I could feel it calling me to come and sit for a while. But my thoughts would immediately pound out a list of other things that needed my attention more. So, I'd pass by the room to attend to my other responsibilities. This same scenario would play out day after day. I looked at that chair for days, but just couldn't find the time or the motivation to sit. This may sound ridiculous, but the struggle was real.

Thankfully, the books I was reading on Christian meditation kept me in the game. I'm forever grateful to the many authors for their inspiration and encouragement to sit with God. It was so tempting to just give up. But the Holy Spirit gently nudged me to sit, and finally I was able to work it into my daily routine. Now, after twenty-two years, I am grateful for the loving, patient support from our Lord. He opened a way for me to come closer to Him and I want to share my journey with you.

I recall my own experience when God invited me to a deeper, closer relationship with Him. My story, leading to the founding of the Christian Meditation Center, began many years ago. It was shortly after my first marriage; Pastor Paul came to our house for a visit. He was the pastor of a non-denominational church a friend of ours attended. During the visit, he helped me see how much I needed the salvation Jesus would bring to my life. He told me that if I believed Jesus died for my sins all my sins were forgiven, He would come and live within me and make me whole! Well, at the age of 22, the one thing I knew I wanted and needed was to be made whole. So, I said the Sinner's Prayer[2] and asked Jesus to come and live in my heart. Inviting Jesus Christ to make my life right was the single most important decision I have ever made.

With the help of the Holy Spirit, my eyes were now open, and I could see the error of my ways. It was obvious my lifestyle needed an overhaul. I smoked a pack and a half of cigarettes a day, drank too much beer, didn't eat the right foods, didn't exercise, and wasn't motivated to finish college. These were just the top five of my behavioral challenges. In short, I was a mess. Within a three-year period, I had lost several family members to lifestyle-related deaths. I knew they could have lived healthier, more productive lives if they had taken better care of themselves. It seemed as if everyone in my family drank alcohol and smoked cigarettes. I knew if I wanted my children to have a shot at not picking up these unhealthy habits, I needed to be a good role model for them.

My journey towards wholeness began with trusting God. I believed that somehow God would accomplish this in me. I knew I would be free from those things that adversely affected my mind, body, and soul. I felt confident in the Bible's promise, "So if the Son sets you free, you are free indeed."[3] I truly believed this would be my reality someday. But I found desiring freedom was only the beginning. The hard work, yet most rewarding, comes to those who are willing to allow God to work in them in any way He deems necessary. The transformation required a commitment to allow God to remove anything unhealthy that kept me from realizing who He created me to be. It wasn't just a process of removing what was no longer needed, it was also about adding the truth of who I truly am and all that comes with that knowledge.

I had spent a lifetime creating who I had become. Most of my thoughts and behaviors were constructed to protect myself from fear and pain, although, ironically, they caused most of both fear and pain in my life. As my relationship with God grew deeper, there came a time I realized what I created no longer served my best interest. The old needed to leave so who God made me to be—could be revealed. I had a strong desire to experience freedom. Freedom, for me, meant nothing was keeping me in bondage any longer. I yearned to have the power to make positive, healthy choices consistently. I knew it might take some time to get there but knew it would be well worth the wait.

My religious experience is broad. I was christened Methodist and later, when I was a teenager, my neighbor took me to a Methodist church a few times. Since I didn't have a strong preference on which church to be married in and my first husband did, we were married in a Catholic church. I attended classes to become Catholic. After we were married, we had a change of heart and decided to start attending a non-denominational church. Two years later when we moved, we started attending a Southern Baptist Church. I also attended an Assembly of God church for six months. After our divorce, I moved and started attending a

Methodist church. It was in this church I met my husband Bill, and we have been there ever since.

As you can see, I have been exposed to several Christian denominations and have learned much from all of them. Each one emphasized a different aspect of the Christian faith. For example, the Catholics have a strong traditional background, while the Southern Baptist's emphasis is on teaching the Word of God. The Assembly of God churches emphasize the work of the Holy Spirit, and I have found the Methodist religion to be methodical, Spirit-filled, with an emphasis on spiritual practices. The exposure to all these denominations has given me a balanced faith perspective and has strengthened my relationship with our Lord. And yet, the transformation was still incomplete.

Fast forward seventeen years, and I am still waiting. I still found myself dealing with obstacles preventing me from having a closer relationship with God. I was really struggling with painful emotional issues and a lifelong addiction to alcohol. I felt frustrated and defeated because in some areas of my life, I was compromising my values. Frankly, at times, I felt unworthy to be called a child of God. Although there had been many victories, such as going back to college, graduating, quitting smoking, experiencing healing within some close relationships, learning how to eat right, exercising on a regular basis, and spiritual breakthroughs, I was still unable to feel right with God. I wanted to feel whole and in control of my thoughts and actions. This may sound unrealistic, but I knew it was possible because the scriptures told me so. I wanted my reality to mirror the Fruit of the Spirit, being love, joy, peace, patience, kindness, goodness, faithfulness, gentleness, and self-control.

In my discouragement, I had what I'd call my *Coming to Jesus* meeting. I prayed about my disappointment and dissatisfaction with how slowly He was moving in my life. I even questioned whether experiencing wholeness was even attainable. Was it possible I'd one day *not* desire alcohol and be free from emotional turmoil? I'd spent so many years chasing the idea, but was it really possible that I could be whole? But here I was, years later, still coping with two of the five issues I'd asked the Lord to heal: drinking alcohol and lingering unresolved emotional issues with my first love.

Well, the answer finally came! One day sitting in my family room, God made it clear to me he wanted me to spend time with Him in stillness and silence! There were no words;

it was a subtle knowing. It was more like I sensed He was calling me to a closer relationship with Him. Thus began my journey to experience the interior presence of God.

I was aware of others who had experienced this calling on their lives. I was drawn to many Christian authors that wrote about contemplation, meditation, quiet prayer, centering prayer, and other prayer genres associated with the practice of just being still and quiet before the Lord.

After months of settling into the idea, I began a regular practice of resting in the Lord by moving my attention away from my thoughts and just focusing on my breathing. During this time, I learned to stay open to allow God to move in me any way He saw fit. I started to see amazing positive changes in my personality and demeanor. People began to comment on the peace and the calmness they saw in my life. I no longer had obsessive thoughts that defeated me emotionally.

After I had been practicing for several years, I attended an eight-day retreat sponsored by Contemplative Outreach. Their organization was founded by Thomas Keating[4], who had played a significant role in introducing a practice called Centering Prayer. Christian meditation and Centering Prayer are both practices to move us into the Kingdom of

God. The retreat offered three hours of meditation spread out over the course of a day for eight days. I was looking forward to spending time with God, uninterrupted, and focusing on just resting in His presence. The first day of the retreat was as I expected, sitting in a peaceful environment to focus only on Him. The second day brought something unexpected; I started crying and it continued for nearly twenty-four hours before it completely stopped. It felt like a soul cleanse. Afterwards, I felt lighter and happier. The rest of the retreat was like the first day, resting in stillness. Attending this retreat was an important part of my journey to wholeness. I knew I would come back.

It was two weeks after the retreat, I had just awakened and was heading to the kitchen for my morning coffee. As I entered, I stopped in front of the coffee pot. To my amazement, I had this *knowing* I would never drink beer or coffee again. I was overwhelmed with gratefulness to God because I had waited so long for this day. I knew I would never drink beer again. Coffee seemed like a consolation prize but one that was happily accepted.

Six months later, I still wasn't drinking beer, nor did I have any desire to do so. But the crazy idea surfaced that maybe having an occasional glass of wine was alright. It started as one or two in the evenings, to take the edge off from working all day. But, as time went on, I increased to four or five glasses a night. I was functioning fine in all areas of my life, but as I was getting older, I felt my sharpness and productivity diminishing. I wanted to stop drinking but couldn't do it alone.

To make a long story short, by the grace of God, I successfully stop drinking alcohol completely in 2010. The Lord directed me to a Christian recovery group where I spent five years supporting and being supported by fellow sojourners who wanted to maintain sobriety. Little did I know how much I would discover about myself during this experience. For example, God showed me that pride was a stronghold in my life, and it was keeping me in bondage. The revelation that it was even an issue for me was surprising. Pride is insidious, and it distorts our Christian witness by glorifying the self. I repented and asked God to remove the pride and give me the gift of humility instead.

I have written the story of my lingering unresolved emotional issues with my first love. In 2014, the Lord called me to write the book *Making Love: The Spiritual Act of Love*.

The book details my love story including my forty-year journey with my first love and the other men I love as well. In short, the unresolved issue with my first love was that I still loved him while married to my first husband. I am sure you can see why I needed God's help to sort it out.

At this point in my journey, I realized that all those things that kept me bound no longer existed for me. He removed the desire to drink alcohol and through His peace I was finally able to overcome the addiction. My feelings for my first love stabilized, and I was able to have honoring thoughts about him and our past relationship. Our life journey is not smooth sailing. God has His own agenda; He knows what we need even when we are not happy with how things are going. As I shared before, the journey towards wholeness is well worth the wait. It feels as though my DNA has changed. My demeanor is different, and my life perspective has matured. I now enjoy the ability of not being tethered to anything. I am no longer a slave to my wayward desires. I now live a true life of freedom.

The truth is—we are not bound to the life we have created, either intentionally or not. I am evidence of that fact. Even my parents stopped drinking, smoking, and started eating better. Sometimes people have to see what other people can do before they can see it or do it for themselves. Unfortunately, this was not the case for my sister. I lost my sister to alcohol addiction when she died at age thirty-two from cirrhosis of the liver. It is painfully difficult to realize that not all of us will experience our freedom in Christ while we are alive, but it is imperative that we live in Hope of that possibility.

For me, Christian meditation, the practice of being still and quiet in the presence of God, accelerated my transformation in Christ. And not just me, but a Cloud of Witnesses who have traversed this path have found it to be true as well. My belief is you too can be healed from the issues in your life and find the same peace and freedom.

God placed a yearning in my heart to share this path to a closer relationship with Him. I realized that God was about to use me for His Will and was directing me on a journey to find a way to share the path of Christian meditation with others. It would take twelve years of praying before God showed me what He had in mind.

CHAPTER 1

The Practice of Christian Meditation

Through the study of books one seeks God; by meditation one finds him. – Padre Pio

One afternoon, a friend texted me and asked how to practice Christian meditation. I thought the instructions might be too long to put into a text as at the time texting was limited to 160 characters. But I did it! Not long after I sent the text,

God placed it on my heart to start a non-profit organization to serve as a vehicle to teach His people how to meditate and develop a closer relationship with Him. I also had the clear impression that He wanted the organization to be called the Christian Meditation Center. I was so excited and at the same time I couldn't believe I didn't see it coming. My career experience included working for a non-profit organization, working at high levels in four for-profit businesses and being responsible for organizing the startup of several others. And yet, it didn't occur to me this would be an ideal way to share the practice of meditation with others. It just goes to show you, God is always in control. I am thankful the idea didn't come from me. It would have given me reason to doubt this was what He wanted for His children.

So, on February 22, 2012, the Christian Meditation Center was formed. I invited other Christ-minded brothers and sisters to share the transformational power of Christian meditation with anyone who wanted to have a more intimate relationship with God. This is our mission, and our vision is to see our families, friends and neighbors integrating meditation into their daily lives to foster a deeper relationship with God. We see church congregations returning to the practice of meditating as an integral part of their Christian faith.

For those of you who want to get started right away, I am ready to dive into the instructions on how to practice. I can appreciate your enthusiasm. I also want to encourage you to consider reading the following chapters as well. They will be a big support in helping you understand this beautiful practice of resting in our Lord and may serve as an encouragement to keep your practice going.

I have been studying and practicing Christian meditation since 2000 and teaching it since 2013. The hardest and possibly the saddest part about teaching this to others is hearing that meditation is too difficult. They say things like, "I can't stay focused," "my thoughts are consuming me," or "I can't just sit for 20 minutes and do nothing." The truth is these are legitimate statements. Let me frame them from a different perspective.

Our thinking mind has reigned throughout our lives and has been allowed to provide input, good and bad, all the while. Most of us don't give it a second thought that maybe we shouldn't allow it so much airtime. But maybe we should, given how our thoughts have a direct impact on our feelings, attitudes, and behaviors. Well, the good news is, that meditation can really help us gain some control back by giving your mind a break. This happens when we give it something else to do. We are going to change where we place our attention. Instead of letting it run wild, we are going to bring our attention into the Kingdom of God, into the center of our being. It is where we will rest for a while.

A good analogy is the way in which our televisions work. We can watch two programs at the same time. You have a full screen that you are watching, but also have a small screen you can still get involved in if you want to, at the top of the screen. Let's call the top screen our thinking mind and the large screen the Kingdom of God. Even though our thinking mind doesn't have our attention, we will notice it still functions. It will continue to remind us of things we need to do, reminisce about the past, and provide commentary on a hot issue…the list goes on for all the things our mind wants to distract us with. It will feel like the goal for our thinking mind is to take back control and become the full screen again. But our goal is to keep our interest and attention on the full screen without getting distracted with the top screen. Although it is possible to maintain our attention and not get distracted, it is easier said than done. The struggle is real; we will find our attention is often kidnapped, and we will start engaging our thoughts. This is normal for almost everyone, so consider yourself among good company. Our goal is not to empty the mind but acknowledge thoughts without engaging them. We become the observer. Over time, we will find the distractions less and less bothersome.

The truth is we don't have to pay attention to what it is doing. If you find you have inadvertently allowed the small screen to become the full screen, redirect your attention so you move back to the right screen. This redirecting or returning should be done with a gentle, non-judgmental attitude. It doesn't help to get upset or discouraged. We don't want to give more material to the mind to work with. Just recognize it as part of the process and have compassion for yourself, as you return to your original intention to rest in the presence of God. Consider the experience as a commercial, as a brief interruption to the show you are watching. With practice, you will eventually feel more like you are watching paid TV where there are little to no commercials.

Remember, you are returning to our Lord every time you find yourself distracted. How many times in your daily life do you return your thoughts and heart to God? So, it is a beautiful thing, even if you have to return to Him one hundred times a day. Consider your meditation practice as a powerful way to anchor yourself in our Lord.

There are several ways to practice Christian meditation. I practice and teach only one way. My preference is to keep it simple, so it can be incorporated into an already busy schedule. You will find my practice at the end of this chapter. It doesn't matter how you find your way to the Kingdom of God, just find a way to meditate that works for you. You may find it easier to incorporate the practice into your prayer time, scripture reading, daily devotions or journaling. It is easiest to meditate any time you are experiencing God from your heart. Praying is a good launch into meditation. Since you are already with Him, just stop the talking or activity and remain in His Presence in silence. Then linger there for a while and *be still and know He is God.*[5] It is a good idea to establish a daily habit with your meditation practice.

Allowing for at least 20 minutes will help your mind and body to settle down. Ideally, spending this time twice a day would certainly be beneficial. However, most of us don't have time to meditate twice a day. What is most important is you spending time in the Kingdom every day. If you miss days, don't be hard on yourself. You lose nothing from missing days and gain much by beginning again.

My personal practice is a combination of several other teachings on how to enter the Kingdom of God. The one teaching that inspired me the most was from the book, *The Cloud of Unknowing,* written anonymously in the latter half of the 14th century. The author provides specific instructions on how we should enter God's presence.

Lift up your heart to God with a gentle stirring of love... Don't let anything else run through your mind and will. Here's how. Forget what you know. Forget everything God made and everybody who exists and everything that's going on in the world, until your thoughts and emotions aren't focused on or reaching toward anything, not in a general way and not in any particular way. Let them be. For the moment, don't care about anything.[6]

It is fairly easy to lift our heart to God with a gentle stirring of love, but not let anything else run through our mind is far from easy. Don't let this discourage you. I have found, focusing on the love in my heart and noticing my breath going in and out distances my attention from my thoughts. Remember, we need to step away from analyzing our performance. Our analysis puts the focus on us when it should be on God.

Here are some suggestions on how to approach meditation:

1. Believe God desires a deeper and richer relationship with you.

2. Come with no agenda or desire for anything but Him.

3. Make your intention to rest in stillness, silence and the spaciousness of your inner being—the Kingdom of God.

4. Let your attitude be one of attentiveness and love towards God, like a silent worship.

5. Invite Him to do whatever is needed to make you more like Christ.

6. Know, "Being confident of this, that He who began a good work in you will carry it on to completion."[7]

7. Accept, "Therefore, since we are receiving a kingdom that cannot be shaken, let us give thanks, by which we offer to God an acceptable worship with reverence and awe; for indeed our God is a consuming fire."[8]

Indeed, let us be grateful! My hope is that you believe you are ready to take this journey to the Center to find out for yourself what awaits within the Kingdom. I can assure you that you won't be disappointed. I can tell you, for most people it is not an easy discipline to stay with. We are not oriented to be still for long periods of time. If you are task-oriented you may lose your desire to practice, because at times it feels like you aren't doing anything. We may also be discouraged when we find our minds have kidnapped us from our desire to spend time with God. As I already said, whenever that happens, we are to take heart and return our attention back to God. We keep returning, so that one day we will just be there. Maybe this is what Paul had in mind when he gave instruction to "pray without ceasing,"[9] a time when we move from praying to becoming Prayer.

Let's begin with finding a time during the day that works best with your schedule. Find a place where you can meditate without distractions. Decide how you will meditate--will you use a chair, sit, or kneel on the floor or lie down? Keep in mind there isn't a magical way to meditate. Our attention is not on the body; it is on the Kingdom within us. So, it doesn't matter how you position your body. What will matter to you is comfort. I suggest you find a position that is comfortable for you to be in during your meditation time. Then decide how much time you will spend in meditation. It is best to plan enough time for your mind and body to settle down. That is why it is recommended you begin with at least fifteen minutes; twenty minutes is better; thirty minutes is best. You should set a timer, so you won't be distracted with how much longer you have before the meditation ends.

The instructions below offer support for those who are beginners, intermediates, and advanced students.

1. Sit up straight, shoulders back, chest area open, resting your hands comfortably in your lap.

2. Pray *The Lord's Prayer*.

3. Your attitude should be one of gratitude towards life. Lift a prayer of gratitude and thankfulness for all God has provided for you.

4. Pray from your heart and invite God to open your heart and soul to do His will. Surrender your will to His love and care, so He can make you more like Him.

5. To move to resting in Him, we stop talking to Him and remain at our heart center in quietness and stillness. It is important to linger for a while; ideally 20 minutes or more. If you find your attention has strayed, gently return to your heart center and linger some more.

6. If you find it difficult to remain at your heart center, focus on breathing, the breath moving in and out of your lungs, for several minutes. Stay alert and relaxed.

7. You should have an open attentiveness during the meditation. This will help you move into the present moment.

8. Then move your focus on your heart for several minutes. Feel like a child, feel your heart light and full of love. Let go of any thoughts, emotions or images and just unwind.

9. Then go back to focusing on your breathing. If your attention draws you back to your mind, just gently return to your breathing. When you feel ready, return to your heart center.

10. To go deeper into the center of your being, silently say the word, *Deeper*. Remain in the silence and stillness within.

11. At the end of your meditation time, with eyes still closed, take a couple of minutes to bring yourself back to your surroundings.

12. Thank God for all He has done for you during this time together. As you go through the day, bring the peace and calmness you experienced with you.

If you find it challenging to stay motivated by practicing alone, consider a group. The experience of meditating in a group is different and many people prefer it. The Christian Meditation Center offers online group sessions with trained facilitators. The sessions will help keep you accountable to your desire to spend time with God.

My beloved spoke and said to me, "Arise, my darling, my beautiful one, come with me. -Song of Songs 2:10

CHAPTER 2

The Practice of Surrender

Your kingdom come, Your will be done, on earth as it is in Heaven. [10]

The primary purpose of surrendering our will to God's Will is to be transformed into the likeness of Christ. This may make you feel uneasy. We may wonder, "What does that mean, exactly?" When we don't know what our future looks like, we tend to be uncertain about what we are willing to commit our time and energy to.

What helped me surrender my will to His Will, was my life at the time. As I had shared in the Prologue—I was a mess! If you have read my memoir, *Making Love: The Spiritual Act of Love*, you know what I am saying. It was the realization that what I was producing in my life was pitiful. I felt, "What do I have to lose?" So, with the faith of a mustard seed,[11] I surrendered with the hope He would provide the life He intended for me.

To lay the foundation, we need to have belief, grace, and faith. These essentials remind me of what I need to return to when I find myself moving through life from my own will, my own pattern of living. Although my own will brings a sense of comfort and something familiar, it does not produce the life God wants for me. So, I need to surrender or change my mind and place myself back into God's care, believing He can be trusted to complete the work He had started in me. The biggest lesson I have learned over the years is by desiring God's Will for my life, without question is what I want as well!

Wanting God's Will is just the beginning point in the transition into the new way of living. Christian meditation provides a daily experience where we can practice surrendering our will to His Will. When we find our mind has distracted us and we become engaged with our thoughts, we gently bring ourselves back to the Kingdom of God, the Center of our being—into God's care. You can use the term Mind of Christ interchangeably with the Kingdom of God if it's helpful. Basically, we are moving from our mind to the Mind of Christ. The latter will allow us to align our will with God's Will. We approach this from our spiritual selves, not from our imaginations. We will explore this more in Chapter 6. For now, we will briefly touch on the essentials of surrender.

BELIEF

Let's take a peek into the Bible to discover God's plan for our future—a promise of positive change. To be more specific, He wants to bring us back to a time before all the mess started, a place of new beginnings. You will notice throughout this book I reference scripture quite a bit. For me, scripture is medicine for my soul. I do recall the years when I first became a Christian and didn't appreciate it in the same way. Other Christians would quote scripture and I would politely say, "Just tell me in your own words." Frankly, I didn't understand what the scripture was saying, but the person sharing it would say it in a way that made it clearer. As I grew in the Lord, the Bible made more sense. Today I still find it a great companion for understanding Truth. With that said, let's see what the LORD says:

> "When seventy years are completed for Babylon, I will come to you and fulfill my good promise to bring you back to this place. "For I know the plans I have for you," declares the LORD, "plans to prosper you and not to harm you, plans to give you hope and a future. Then you will call on me and come and pray to me, and I will listen to you. You will seek me and find me when you seek me with all your heart. I will be found by you," declares the LORD, "and will bring you back from captivity."[12]

Although this scripture is describing a promise to bring the Israelites out of Babylon to the promised land, a physical location, this is also a picture of how God will bring you and me into our promised land, the Kingdom of God, spiritual location. He wants to restore our soul and bring us back to Himself.

We may think we'll accept the invitation when our life is in better shape; after we clean up our act some.

We find in the book of Acts that, *"God did this so that they would seek him and perhaps reach out for him and find him, though he is not far from any one of us."*[13] In one sense, how comforting to know He is not far from any one of us. The invitation is available anytime, *"Come near to God and He will come near to you."*[14] Yet, it may feel a little scary at the same time. It's normal to feel this way. We may not feel we are good enough or we are afraid we won't live up to God's expectations. We may think we'll accept the invitation *when* our life is in better shape, *after* we clean up our act. Yet, there is so much to discover about ourselves along the way. The best and more complete discovery comes when we invite God to come along with us. We grow the most through the doing, not the done state.

The truth is He takes us just as we are. *He knows everything about us, even the number of hairs on our head.*[15] *He formed us in our mother's womb.*[16] *His love for us is boundless.* [17] *He is patient with us.* [18] I have experienced His gracious and merciful love and patience. And although we want to put on the best version of something we think God wants, He is primarily interested in our desire for a relationship with Him. He wants you to want Him. So how do we do that? It is quite simple; we open our heart, and we ask. The Good News is that no one is turned down, NO ONE!

This is the prayer I prayed in my early 20's. It changed the direction of where my life was going.

Father, I know that I have broken your laws and my sins have separated me from you. I am truly sorry, and now I want to turn away from my past sinful life toward you. Please forgive me and help me avoid sinning again. I believe that your Son, Jesus Christ died for my sins, was resurrected from the dead, is alive, and hears my prayer. I invite Jesus to become the Lord of my life, to rule and reign in my heart from this day forward. Please send your Holy Spirit to help me obey You, and to do Your will for the rest of my life. In Jesus' name I pray. Amen.

If you prayed this prayer, you are now a child of God. Welcome to the Kingdom of God! You have decided to let God transform you into the original version of yourself: the version He created.

Let me share with you some exciting and amazing facts about what you have inherited and who you are moving forward. Your identity is now in Jesus Christ and Heaven has been restored to you. *When you invited Christ to live in your heart, He was already there, but your invitation made Him alive within you.* Now that He is alive, you have received the fullness of the Godhead and you have been made complete in Him.[19] The Godhead is referring to the nature of God, especially as it exists in three persons —the Father, Son and Holy Spirit, or, the Trinity.

So, what is this fullness you have received? Jesus says, *"I am the light of the world! The one who follows me will never walk in darkness but will have the light of life."*[20] This transformation from darkness to light is crucial for our wellbeing. If we decide to continue on the same old path, we will find ourselves managing both our internal and external darkness. Unfortunately, we will also be doomed to create the same type of experiences. Experiences, in the beginning, promise happiness and end in disillusionment and despair. Your decision to follow Jesus has changed the course of your life. It is through Him we find true happiness.

GRACE

Grace was given to us in Christ Jesus before the beginning of time, so God could fulfill His own purpose in and through us.[21] We can define grace as a holy covering He freely provides as we develop our relationship with Him. *Specifically, it is the extension of God's power working in us*[22]. *Grace flows from the fullness of Christ.*[23] *It is the full provision for us to do the work of God.*[24] *It is the power that keeps us saved.*[25] *Working outside of grace to maintain salvation is a worthless effort.*[26] *Grace emboldens us to draw near to God.*[27] *And finally, He is able to save completely those who come to God through Him, because He always lives to intercede for them.*[28] Grace keeps us in right standing with God. It allows God to see us through Christ. When He looks at us, He sees Christ, Christ's perfection. What is most important about grace is that it is a pure gift; you cannot do anything to receive grace and *it is freely given to you.*[29] Our role is to receive it by faith.

Thomas Merton sums it up like this, *"Grace is not a strange, magic substance, which is subtly filtered into our souls to act as a kind of spiritual penicillin. Grace is unity, oneness with ourselves, oneness with God. Grace is the peace of friendship with God and if it does not necessarily bring us to a felt peace, it nonetheless gives us every reason to be at peace. If we could only understand and appreciate what it means. Grace means that there is no opposition between man and God, and that man is able to be sufficiently united with himself to live without opposition to God. Grace is friendship with God."[30]*

FAITH

Faith is the foundation for our participation in the Kingdom of God. The Word of God tells us, *"Therefore, since we have been justified through faith, we have peace with God through our Lord Jesus Christ, through whom we have gained access by faith into this grace in which we now stand. And we boast in the hope of the glory of God."[31] "So let us draw near to God with a sincere heart and with the full assurance that faith brings, having our hearts sprinkled to cleanse us from a guilty conscience and having our bodies washed with pure water.*"[32] *In Him and through faith in Him we may approach God with freedom and confidence.*[33] Faith provides access to the Kingdom, and we have an invitation to visit often. The practice of Christian meditation is a way to accept the invitation to spend time with Him. This practice provides the guidance we need to discover our Center.

It is not easy to continue to practice if we are unsure that what we are doing is in fact doing anything at all.

Faith and hope go together like peanut butter and jelly. Scripture defines it this way, *"Faith is confidence in what we hope for and assurance about what we do not see."*[34] As we practice meditation, we will rely on both faith and hope. First, we need to have faith and a sure hope that our practice is transforming us into the likeness of Christ. It is not easy to continue to practice if we are unsure that what we are doing is in fact doing anything at all.

I spent several months reading about Christian meditation before I started to actually practice it. Still, it was so hard for me to just sit there with no agenda, other than spending time with our Lord. When I began my practice, I was optimistic and motivated. God gave me some consolations early on in my practice, so I felt Him with me. I will describe them in more detail in chapter three. However, there were also times when I did not feel His presence with me at all. I started to question my initial desire to practice. But the primary reason I continued, is because of the people who had authored books talked about their own experience and by others who I knew were practicing. *It is important to be mutually encouraged by each other's faith.*[35] To say the least, they kept me motivated.

I remember a time when I went to see Thomas Keating. He was speaking at a church and was available to anyone who wanted a signed copy of his new book. Those that attended had the opportunity to meet with him privately for a minute or two. I do not remember anything I said, but I do remember everything he said. He told me to continue with my practice and to not give up. I took his advice, and I am so grateful I did. I share this story because it is easy to give up. We need faith and hope as we move through the days, months, and years. We need to remember we have a sure hope if we remain faithful to our desire to come closer to God. It's important to know we may have times when our faith will go into hiding.

Well, how do we deal with a waning faith? The answer is, we take heart because we are in good company. Jesus spent a lot of time building up his disciple's faith. There are several examples in the Bible where Jesus admonished them about not having enough faith. On one occasion, Jesus is on a boat with his disciples and the winds pick up and the waves are getting dangerously high. The account of the story called it a furious storm and Jesus is fast asleep. His disciples are understandably freaking out. *"They woke Him up and said to Him, "Lord, save us! We're going to drown!" He replied, "You of little faith, why are you so afraid?" Then he got up and rebuked the winds and the waves, and it was completely calm. The men were amazed and asked, "What kind of man is this? Even the winds and the waves obey him!"* [36]

This story should encourage us not to lose heart. Even his disciples had their moments of fear and uncertainty. So, it shouldn't surprise us if we become afraid or doubtful. During those times, we should remember we are called *"To live by faith, not by sight."*[37] There is also a promise I cling to when I find my faith waning, *"Jesus is the Author and the Finisher of our faith."*[38] And I find comfort in these scriptures, *"If we are faithless, he remains faithful, for He cannot disown Himself."*[39] He has made it simple for us to expand our faith; all we have to do is ask Him to increase it.[40]

Faith plays a significant role in whether we will continue the practice of Christian meditation. I want to encourage you, as I did, to lean on the faith of others when you do not feel the practice is worthwhile. It is important to believe that it is impossible to be in God's presence without having been exposed to *the Fruit of the Spirit*.[41] It's not possible to be in His presence without having an eternal residue left in us. When we meditate, we are exposed to Eternity and are present with the Father, Son and Holy Spirit. God's presence transforms our identity and heals our mind, our heart, and our soul. The next chapter shows how we can participate within the practice of presence.

Presence

Have you ever seen lovers gaze into each other's eyes,

or sit silently, looking out over the ocean?

No words are necessary.

In fact, they just seem to get in the way.

As love draws us deeper into the oneness of our hearts,

our two hearts begin to beat as one

as we breathe together. So it is with old friends.

Just their mere presence means everything to us.

Everything else is lost in the moment we're together.

It's like this with silence. As we enter and dwell together with God,

no words are necessary.

Our hearts begin to beat as one.

Our spirits mingle in a mutual dwelling of God

in us and us in God.

This is what restoration is all about...

God's restoring our original intent,

the profound mystery of wholeness, oneness,

the unity of belonging, presence, and rest.

We are like lovers and old friends

who yearn to sit and dwell with the Holy One

in this vast mystery of eternity.

Enter in, Come cross the threshold

Come, let us enter in.

~ Bob Holmes

CHAPTER 3

The Practice of Presence

For in Him we live and move and have our being.[42]

We experience the Presence of God when we turn our attention to God. He is everywhere! The only way to miss Him is to hide from Him or forget to bring Him along. There are any number of ways to experience his presence, including: praying, reading your Bible, singing, and journaling, to name a few. This is a very short list. You can find Him in any activity you are doing, as long as you are choosing to allow Him to join you. Most of us feel comfortable and understand His desire to meet with us in the outward circumstances of our daily life. But for some of us, we find it more difficult to understand that He is also interested in participating in our inner life. This chapter is devoted to His presence within us. We know He resides there because Jesus told us, *"Nor will they say, 'See here!' or 'See there!' For indeed, the kingdom of God is within you."*[43]

Paul in his letter to the Church in Corinth was aware of this truth when he posed this question, *"Do you not know that you are the temple of God and that the Spirit of God dwells in you?"*[44] And we find Jesus comforting the disciples before He ascended into heaven saying, *"And surely I am with you always, to the very end of the age."*[45] One last scripture I will share, one where Paul affirms His presence within us, *"Here there is no Gentile or Jew, circumcised or uncircumcised, barbarian, Scythian, slave or free, but Christ is all, and is in all."*[46] These scriptures also show us another amazing truth, not just God, but Christ and the Holy Spirit are within us too. What treasures we possess!

So, if the Holy Three live within us, why are we not like them? It seems we should have our act together a little more than we do. I remember reading Galatians, Chapter 5, wanting so much to understand how in the world to walk by the Spirit. Let's read it together:

> *You, my brothers and sisters, were called to be free. But do not use your freedom to indulge the flesh; rather, serve one another humbly in love. For the entire law is fulfilled in keeping this one command: "Love your neighbor as yourself." If you bite and devour each other, watch out or you will be destroyed by each other.*
>
> *So I say, **walk by the Spirit**, and you will not gratify the desires of the flesh. For the flesh desires what is contrary to the Spirit, and the Spirit what is contrary to the flesh. They are in conflict with each other, so that you are not to do whatever you want. But if you are led by the Spirit, you are not under the law.[47]*

So, there it is in verse 16, "walk by the Spirit." The King James version translates this as "walk in the Spirit." Frankly, the translation didn't matter, I was unable to do either. I read several books to try to figure it out, but they didn't help, or I wasn't able to understand what I was supposed to do. Either way I was not doing it and found myself repeating patterns that were no longer serving my best interests. As I shared earlier, there was a list of poor lifestyle choices I was involved in, like smoking cigarettes, drinking alcohol, didn't eat right, didn't exercise...do I have to say more? It's enough to say, there was a lot of house cleaning to be done.

There is also the teaching from Jesus, *"Abide in Me, and I in you. As the branch cannot bear fruit of itself, unless it abides in the vine, neither can you, unless you abide in Me."*[48] Sounds like a lovely place to be, abiding in Christ. But how is it possible? How can I sense myself abiding in Christ throughout the day? Occasionally, I would sense Him with me, but *abiding* sounds like we are to be so close all the time.

For many years, the ability to walk in the Spirit and abide in Christ were out of reach for me. It wasn't until I started practicing Christian meditation that it dawned on me to walk in the Spirit and to abide in Christ was directly related to how I was living out my life. Up until then, I was living my life through thoughts. So, some of my thoughts were not based on truth and this led to many errors in judgment. My focus was based primarily on what information my mind was feeding me through the day. Relying on my thoughts attached to misaligned emotions was not a stable way to run my life.

Christian meditation, on the other hand, changes the focus away from your thoughts onto the Center of your being—the Kingdom of God. When we are consistently living from our Source, we are more grounded and more likely to make good decisions. Spending time in the Kingdom stabilizes our emotions, quiets us to hear from God and opens us to so many possibilities that we couldn't imagine for ourselves. As I emphasized earlier, the challenge is we have been oriented our entire lives to live only from our thoughts. We have allowed them to rule us. So, it will take some time before we are able to manage our lives from the Center of our being. I noticed this for myself as I continued to meditate. I noticed I was living more from my Center and this new focus had a positive influence on my thoughts and behaviors.

Once I was armed with this knowledge, it all started to make sense to me. If I want to walk in the Spirit, I need to spend time where the Spirit is—in the center of my being. This is not just an intellectual statement, but one from years of experience of returning to the Kingdom to spend time with the Holy Three. The more I showed up to be with Them, the more I became *like* Them. It is as if the practice of meditation was opening up a portal to the Eternal. During the time we are together, transformation is taking place. I don't always know what is changing, but I notice shifts in my personality. I found I was less likely to lash out at others when I'm frustrated. I found myself feeling more compassionate. People I knew commented on how peaceful and calm I'd been lately. There are many ways God shows up in my everyday experiences.

When we are meditating, we are using our interior eyes to move our attention towards our heart. The Kingdom of God is in this area. Then we stay and linger there for a while. The challenge, however, is our thinking mind will try to draw our attention upward towards our thoughts. This is natural and it is a part of the process. Once we notice our attention has shifted, we gently move back down towards our heart center. This leaving and returning happens throughout the meditation. Thankfully, the Kingdom doesn't lock the door, so we can continue to come and go. This is the practice of Christian meditation.

Let's spend a little time on how to handle distractions. There are always interruptions in our lives. We set out to do one thing and other things get in the way. Disruptions may happen while we are meditating or doing any kind of activity. So how do we handle all these distractions? The best advice I can give is to let them *be*. Whether they are coming from the outside environment, or you find yourself engaged with your thoughts while you are meditating. I understand the frustration of just wanting peace and quiet, but it isn't realistic. It's best to know what we can and can't control. If we let the distractions just *be*, we won't give them any power. But as soon as we start with the inner dialog, "Why does that neighbor need to mow his lawn now?" or "Why am I thinking about Aunt Sally?", we have moved away from our original intention. What we give attention to will move into a position of power and will become what we will focus on. So, notice the distraction, but move your attention back to the Kingdom to maintain your intention to be with God. Eventually, your mind will bother you less and less and you will stay in the Kingdom longer and longer without interruptions.

Maybe this is a good time for another analogy. Let's say you bought a new car because you got a higher paying job. The first thing you want to do is to learn about your new car. You need to learn where the blinkers, windshield wipers, emergency brake, and all the other gadgets are before you start to drive. Once you learn where everything is and how to operate the car, then you are ready to go for a drive.

Let's say your new job is sending you to a new work location and you have never been there before. So, you put on your GPS to guide you there the first couple of times. But after some practice, you don't need the GPS—you know where you are going. For your first several trips to work, you will notice all the things going on outside of your car, like the stores, where the gas stations are and the other cars on the road. Inside your car, you might notice a song on the radio, your thoughts, your feelings, or a bug flying around. But after several weeks, you may notice you are barely paying attention to your surroundings. And after several months, you may stop paying attention all together. You start running on auto pilot. Then one day, you drive into your parking space and think, "How did I get here; I don't remember the trip at all."

The journey with Christian meditation is very similar to the car. We need to first learn about meditation, then we need directions on how to do it. Then we give it a try and may find it takes time to find the Kingdom. Once we find it, we know where it is so the next time the trip is a little easier to navigate. The more we practice meditation, we can go directly to the Kingdom with little difficulty. After many times of entering in, we may meditate and find ourselves there, but can't seem to remember how we got there. This doesn't mean you will always have this experience. The next time you practice, you may find it takes time to settle into the Kingdom. It is best to not have any expectations or goals when you enter in to resting in God's presence. Let love alone *be* your motive for turning to Him.

When we practice Christian meditation, we are preparing a way for God's gift of contemplative prayer. This may sound contrary to when I said, "have no expectations or goals." But it is not. We should not desire to rest in His presence for any personal gain, including desiring consolations from Him. We should recognize we may have more of an interest in something mystical than we do in Him personally. It is always a good idea to check our motives and ask where we are coming from—a place of the ego or the Spirit.

It's important to understand the gift of contemplative prayer. This prayer is given to you from God; you can't do anything to receive it. But Christian meditation provides a beautiful environment for it to take place. It happens when God wants you to experience Himself. God has given this prayer to many people, including me. So, I feel comfortable talking about it. I had once thought I needed to be someone special or saintly to be touched by God in such a personal way. But God is faithful, providing what is needed to strengthen the relationship.

It happened to me rather unexpectedly. I was meditating and suddenly, my mental faculties became suspended. My mind was silent. My body felt completely still. I felt peaceful and loved. Within the center of me, it felt like God was hugging me. It didn't last long, maybe five to ten seconds. It has happened to me three times during different meditation sessions. As you can imagine, this experience affirmed His presence within me...without a doubt.

On another occasion while I was in a group someone else was leading, the facilitator led a meditation, and I went very deep into the center of my being. While I was there, I felt the most profound love. I had never experienced love so intense and palpable. The love was so tender and adoring. It was very personal and relational. It was like the experience of falling in love for the first time, but supersized.

We meditated about twenty minutes. When the facilitator asked us to return our attention to the room, it took me a minute or two. When I did, I was crying. The crying lasted about five minutes. Afterwards, I felt something lasting had happened to me. As the days went by, I noticed that my love for God, others, and myself had deepened. It was truly a God encounter and the benefits from the experience have not faded over time. It has fortified my faith and trust in a truly loving God. Even with all my imperfections, He is with me and loves me.

Although these types of experiences happen to many people, there are others who meditate on a regular basis but never experience any consolations. So, it's important to meditate with a pure desire to only spend time with Him, trusting He is with you—always.

Chapter 4

Practice of Stillness

Close your eyes and follow your breath to the still place that leads to the invisible path that leads you home. -Teresa of Avila

It's easier to sense God's presence when we are experiencing silence and stillness within. It's difficult to readily sense Him when there is a lot of noise in our inward and outward landscapes. Focusing on our breath is a perfect way to move into stillness. We are never more present than when we are paying attention to the breath coming in and going out of our diaphragm. If we can maintain our focus on breathing, we'll find our body becoming still and more relaxed. As our awareness of stillness grows, silence will emerge as a palpable energy, for silence is alive and active within us.

Maintaining our attention on breathing, we will enter into the present moment. The focused attention allows us to *be here now*, which is rarely experienced in everyday life. Most of our awake life is focused on the past or the future. We find our minds drifting even while we are doing ordinary things. When we are not present, we are supplementing our experiences with an alternative reality. If we are focused on the past, we are mentally reliving a reality that is past. It is history and it should be given its proper place, but never at the expense of depriving us of the importance and the sacredness of this moment. We can say the same for the future. When we spend time creating thoughts about what might come later, we need to recognize we are speculating. For there is no way to truly know what will come next. Results from speculating are naturally unstable. We are more effective when we live life in the present moment. The practice of meditation helps us to be present and fully available to deal with situations from a neutral perspective.

This is truly easier said than done. Have you ever been fixated in the past? Have you ever been distracted by a past relationship? Was it a good or bad experience? Do you every now and then replay what happened in your mind? Overtime, doing this could keep you stuck in the past. This happened to me, as my mind was focused on the past, it was dragging my past into the present moment, which in turn brought it into my future. So, how was anything new going to come into my life?

It's impossible to lay a steady framework for a fresh future if we're dragging our past into it. The gift of the present moment brings the possibility of a new life, a clean slate for God to use to recreate and transform us into the likeness of Christ. This is why the *Good News* is such good news! Christ died for our sins, and we are forgiven! We are forgiven everything. This is paramount in establishing a new life in Christ.[49] Forgetting what *lies* behind and reaching forward to what *lies* ahead.[50] What will our future look like if we add new on an old foundation?

Receiving forgiveness can be so hard and for some of us it is a process, not a one-and-done experience. I know I needed more time to heal and move beyond my fixation on my past. And still the good news is God was with me and showed me the importance of why I needed to struggle emotionally before He healed me. There is always a reason when solutions are delayed. But if we are patient, we may find an important lesson in the struggle. The difficulty also pushes us to rely on Him for the answer and for the healing. In the process, our faith and love for Him expands and we're more likely to feel His presence and His love.

So, this new life in Christ happens immediately in the heavenly realm, but it takes time to unfold in time and space. Once I forgave the past and reconciled it in my heart, I was able to love wholeheartedly. I found the love I had was purer and selfless. I was able to extend this new love to those in my past, and just as importantly, to those I would meet along the way. I found that transformation is not a cake walk, but it is well worth whatever is needed to reach higher ground and the freedom to participate in a new life. Even with everything I went through, I wouldn't change a thing.

So, we can see why the practice of stillness is crucial to our journey to wholeness. Like any new skill one wants to acquire, we must practice stillness so that we CAN become still. I haven't met anyone who is inherently still by nature. So, coming inside to focus on our breath provides an easy way to move into stillness and with time possess the ability to remain there. When we become still, it offers an opportunity to experience peace. You might be thinking, "Aren't the two the same thing?" But there are subtle differences. Finding and experiencing stillness is something we do. Once it's discovered, it is an indicator we have found the present moment. Then at some point, stillness moves into peace.

In the inner stillness where meditation leads, the Spirit secretly anoints the soul and heals our deepest wounds.
-St. John of the Cross

Peace is more tangible and possesses a calming and comforting quality we can feel. Peace feels more alive than stillness. We find this peace in Christ.[51] Jesus is even referred to as the Prince of Peace.[52] He gave us His peace; one that will reassure our hearts and calm our fears.[53] Peace comes with power to change us. It may take time to shift from stillness to peace. But once there, you have found your inner sanctuary.

I find silence to be a friend in the process of being still and being present with God.[54] It serves as a buffer for both my thoughts and what is going on outside. However, it is unrealistic to think you can have a noise free environment or that you can blank out your mind. The best defense is to not let the distractions—become a distraction. This morning I was meditating and Peaches, our dog, decided to chew a toy right next to my chair. My first thought was to stop meditating and take her toy away. But I decided to let the distraction *be* and I moved my attention deeper within. Just making a minor change to my attitude and reaction allowed both of us to continue what we were doing. Distractions can teach us many lessons on how to deal with them without the negative thoughts. We can apply these lessons outside of meditation as well. With that said, I still like my environment to be relatively quiet to spend time in silent worship. With time, you will find it much easier to deal with distractions.

Silence is not merely the absence of sound. There is a depth to it, and it has a grounding effect on our being. Silence is not visible, but clearly it exists. We can see its power when we sense the uneasiness in others when there is no sound. More profoundly, God's Word comes from the Eternal and enters through the silence to be heard by the soul.

It is there He provides inspiration, guidance, and transformation.

For God alone my soul waits in silence; from him comes my salvation. -Psalm 62:1

Some of us have lost our connection with silence, leaving a void that is filled up with noise. Losing the connection separates us from a deeper appreciation for life. In silence there is no separation; it is at the core of all things, and it connects everything. It is everywhere, hidden from our senses until the noise subsides. Yet, if we are accustomed to always having sound around us, silence can be intimidating. If you feel this way, you may want to introduce silence slowly. A good start is to turn off the music and television when you are using it for background noise. Sometimes just being aware of how often you can control the amount of silence is beneficial.

Practicing stillness in silence reestablishes a healthy relationship with distractions, provides a respite from our thoughts, strengthens our focus, and stabilizes our emotions. The pair make a perfect couple and play a complementary role in raising our awareness of our inner life. They have the capacity to open a new frontier for us to explore. What is waiting for you?

Chapter 5

The Practice of Prayer

For who is the one who will devote themselves to be close to Me? declares the LORD. [55]

Who is the one who will devote themselves to be close to Me? That sentence repeated in my mind long after I read it. The question made me feel sad. I don't mean to interject my feelings on God, but if it were coming from me, I would be feeling lonely. The question deeply touched my heart. Especially, when I know how much He loves me. He has demonstrated His love time and time again. Yet we are leery about drawing closer to God. Intentionally or not, we tend to distance ourselves from Him.

So why do we keep Him at arm's length when an embrace is all He wants? I suspect there are many reasons, but I feel it comes down to a fear of losing *our* identity. Or we fear interference with *our* plans for the future. The commentary in our head probably sounds like this, "What will other people think about me?" "Will they see me as a Jesus freak?" "What if He wants me to move or change my lifestyle?" "What if He wants me to give more money to support the Church's mission?" On and on we could pound out the excuses. We are perfectly fine to have God in our lives as long as He doesn't intrude too much.

May I suggest another question: "What are we leaving on the table by not coming closer?" If we believe scriptures that tell us what we will receive if we seek restoration and a closer walk with God, the benefits are tremendous. In Jeremiah Chapter 30, the Lord lays out His promises. He will restore our finances, keep our homes safe, increase our family size, bring us honor, restore our health and heal our wounds. Wow, those are amazing promises! But let's not move closer for the benefits. Let's move closer for the Love. *No eye has seen, no ear has heard, and no mind has imagined what God has prepared for those who love him.* [56]

One way to move closer is through prayer. When we pray, we open ourselves to His presence. We open our hearts and allow Him to remove obstacles that place limitations on our relationship. This is certainly what He wants to do. But my experience has shown how limited I am to know what is best for me. Trusting God has our back is key to our prayer life. It reminds me of the story of Joseph. You may remember his eleven brothers didn't like him because he kept telling them about his dreams. Joseph told them they were going to bow down to him one day. This made them very angry, and they schemed to throw him into a large pit and leave him there to die. But then one of the brothers persuaded the others to sell Joseph to some merchants instead. He ends up being sold as an Egyptian slave to one of Pharaoh's officials, Potiphar. He was doing quite well until Potiphar's wife accused him of trying to seduce her, which was not true. Even though just the opposite was true, they threw him in jail anyway. But even through difficult circumstances, Joseph stayed true to God.

It was not long after that happened, Pharaoh threw his cup bearer and baker into jail. While in jail, Joseph interpreted the cup bearer and the baker's dreams. In both their dreams he predicted they would be released from jail. Joseph asked them to remember him after they were released. His predictions came true, and they were released from prison.

Two years later, Pharaoh was having dreams that troubled him and didn't understand what they meant. No one on his staff knew how to interpret the dream. The cupbearer remembered Joseph and told Pharaoh he knew someone who could help him. *So, Pharaoh sent for Joseph, and he was quickly brought from the dungeon. When he had shaved and changed his clothes, he came before Pharaoh. Pharaoh said to Joseph, "I had a dream, and no one can interpret it. But I have heard it said of you that when you hear a dream you can interpret it." "I cannot do it," Joseph replied to Pharaoh, "but God will give Pharaoh the answer he desires." God did give the answer concerning his dream.* [57] The dream was a warning of an impending famine.

Fast forward in the story, Joseph is made second in command of all Egypt, and saves his family from famine, including the eleven brothers who wanted him dead. And this is what he said to them after all those years away and all the hardship he endured, *"You intended to harm me, but God intended it for good to accomplish what is now being done, the saving of many lives."*[58]

Have you prayed for a job, a relationship, or home you wanted, and didn't get it? You were probably disappointed your prayer wasn't answered the way you wanted. And for some of those prayers, have you ever looked back on your life and thought, "Thank God He didn't answer that prayer!" What may look like a good thing to pray at one time often looks different farther down the road. It's because our perspective changes as time passes. There are reasons for unanswered prayers. Sometimes we misinterpret God's will, and if we are honest, our motives are not pure. We may want things to happen to satisfy our own desires, and hope God will line up with our will.

So why pray at all? Should we just bow down to our circumstances and not say anything? Since we don't always know what is best for us, why bother praying at all? *We bother because scripture tells us to not only to pray but to pray often and about everything.*[59] We know Jesus retreated often to pray.[60] He also taught us how to pray.[61] Jesus also told us, *If we asked in faith, we can move a mountain and if you pray as you had already received it, you will have it.*[62] James tells us, *Is anyone among you sick? Let them call the elders of the church to pray over them and anoint them with oil in the name of the Lord.*[63] These scriptures offer guidance on prayer. But the one that offers the most helpful advice is, *"In the same way, the Spirit helps us in our weakness. We do not know what we ought to pray for, but the Spirit himself intercedes for us with groans that words cannot express. And he who searches our hearts knows the mind of the Spirit, because the Spirit intercedes for the saint in accordance with God's will."*[64] Now we are getting closer to knowing how we are to pray.

Results of my prayers over the years have been a hit or miss proposition. When we pray, we are hoping our effort

When I acknowledge my lack of knowing the fullness of a situation and rely on the Holy Spirit to bring my prayer to God perfectly, I have peace with whatever the outcome.

will produce happy outcomes. It is difficult to pray for someone who is ill, only to find out they didn't recover. Or to pray for a friend's marriage that ends in divorce. Or to pray for direction in my own life, without receiving a reply. I am not going to tell you why prayer at times seems ineffectual, for we have been told otherwise.[65] What I have noticed is, when I acknowledge my limited perspective of a situation and rely on the Holy Spirit to bring my prayer to God perfectly, I have peace with whatever the outcome! This takes the emphasis off my ability, and places it squarely on the One with the power to provide the correct answer to meet the need. I no longer judge the outcomes of my prayers. I love a quote from Tracy McMillan, "Everything will work out in the end, and if it has not worked out yet, then it is not the end."

Speaking in tongues is another form of prayer. It is a gift of the Holy Spirit.[66] This prayer seems more reliable than our attempts at talking to God in our language. Those who speak in tongues are lifting up requests directed by the Holy Spirit. We can stand confident our heartfelt desires are being heard and translated appropriately to meet the person's need.

Then there is the silent prayer of the heart, where we lift up the person or situation we are praying for to the Throne of Grace. We say nothing. We just hold them lovingly in our heart and bring them into the presence of God. This prayer works well, either before or after the practice of Christian meditation. For we already have our attention on Him. We can see from Jesus' teaching why this approach is effective:

> *"But when you pray, go into your room, close the door and pray to your Father, who is unseen. Then your Father, who sees what is done in secret, will reward you. And when you pray, do not keep on babbling like pagans, for they think they will be heard because of their many words. Do not be like them, for your Father knows what you need before you ask him."*[67]

This teaching instructs us to take time to pray in a private place. We find it makes the Father happy if we pray, because He says He will reward us. And He tells us we don't need to have long prayers, for our Father knows what we need before we ask Him. I want to be available and have a desire to be with Him, whether talking out loud, speaking in tongues, or from the silence of my heart. My consent allows Him to come to me. It is there He meets me in my place of innocence secured for me by Jesus, a place where I am free and untethered to anything other than the sacred. A place where only Light remains.

It is in this place He speaks to us. We would benefit greatly to take time to listen. Prayer is not a one-sided conversation. Think about how one sided our relationships would be if we did all the talking and didn't leave time for the other person to respond. It wouldn't be much of a relationship, would it? Consider all the men and women who have heard the Voice of God throughout the ages. So much would have been lost if they hadn't been willing to listen. Are you ready to listen? Jesus has extended the invitation, "Here I am! I stand at the door and knock. If anyone hears my voice and opens the door, I will come in and eat with that person, and they with me."[68]

The practice of Christian meditation provides the other side of the conversation, a way to listen. Once you have spoken to God, stop talking and stay quietly attentive to Him. Let your words go and be open to receive from Him. Responses from God are not always audible. Let the experience of spending time with Him, and your desire to hear Him, be enough. Sometimes He answers in other ways. So, if you are waiting for a healing, restoration of a relationship, justice, children, a financial breakthrough, or anything else, lean on David's confidence when he said, "Lord, I wait for you; you will answer, Lord my God."[69]

Chapter 6

The Practice of Renewing our Mind

Do not conform to the pattern of this world, but be transformed by the renewing of your mind. Then you will be able to test and approve what God's will is—his good, pleasing and perfect will. [70]

Anyone who has spent time reading the Bible is aware there is a difference in the values God and His Kingdom call us to pursue and those the world holds valuable. Once we accept and acknowledge the salvation that comes through Jesus Christ, we are invited into the process of transformation and renewal, which involves switching from living in the kingdom of self to living in the Kingdom of God. This process involves changing our mind about how we will live. Our role is to desire the transformation and be willing. The Holy Spirit is the One who will make the changes.

There were many times my prayer was, "Lord, make me willing." I was far more comfortable living in my kingdom. I know the layout better and have designed many ways to get what I want. Though the Kingdom of God sounds so enticing, it also sounds difficult to reach. But my heart was softened by His words, *"I will instruct you and teach you in the way you should go; I will counsel you with my loving eye on you."*[71] It was difficult for me not to bend towards His teaching. My understanding of how we receive this knowledge comes by relying on His guidance through the Mind of Christ. Our role is to be open to receive what we need from Him.

When we consent to renewing our mind, we are actively participating in what Jesus' prayer is asking the Father to do, *"Your Kingdom Come. Your will be done, on earth as it is in Heaven."*[72] Holiness comes when we bring Heaven to earth. It amazes me how He wants to use us, through Christ, to do this work.[73] We catch glimpses of Heaven as we begin our transfer from one residence to the other. They say, "I once was blind, but now I see" is more accurately stated at, "I once was blind, but now I squint." For when we first enter the Kingdom of God, it takes time for our eyes to adjust to the Light.

The clarity of our sight is determined by how much truth we have accepted. Truth is the essence of Christ. It takes time for us to become accustomed to this new life. We know the fullness of God is in Christ and we have the capacity for the fullness to reside within us as well.[74] However, our sight is temporarily distorted and diminished. But as we take in and accept truth, we will experience the fullness of Christ developing within us. For we know that Christ is the way, the truth, and the life.[75] Eventually, we will see what is true through the eyes of Christ.

I want to share some observations in people that you may have seen as well. I have noticed that people with low levels of truth, also have low levels of understanding. Generally, they suffer with high levels of fear and anxiety. Unfortunately, they also are bombarded with negative emotions such as shame, guilt, depression, and anger. If this is your experience, you are primarily operating from the natural self, dominated by fear. But if you are willing to believe the truth that comes from God, the fullness of Christ will expand within you, offering instead a life governed by love. You can see we are at a great disadvantage if the amount of truth we have is low. The good news is that if we continue to renew our mind, we can rise above negative emotions to more positive ones, such as courage, hope, optimism, love, joy, and peace. Truth heals our mind, body and soul. We are happier and more content when we are bolstered by truth. Truth raises our understanding of who we truly are in Christ and helps us deal effectively with life situations.

I have also noticed a direct correlation between how much truth we possess and how we approach life. If you are on the low end, you will feel that other people are responsible for making your life miserable. You feel like a victim at the hands of other people. As your truth meter rises you will find you have more control and are doing things to support a good life. You feel hopeful that you can turn your life around. The more you renew your mind with truth, the more Christ will work through you. We all know people God is using in a mighty way. Then there are those who have experienced the fullness of Christ and are serving society as an avatar for Him. These are people like you and me who decided to renew their mind by seeking Truth above all else.

Reading scripture is another way to renew our mind and gain Truth. We know God is responsible for the content of the Bible. It's why we call it the *Word of God*. Timothy tells us, *"All Scripture is God-breathed and is useful for teaching, rebuking, correcting and training in righteousness, so that the servant of God may be thoroughly equipped for every good work."*[76] We can trust what the Word of God tells us when it's read from the Holy Spirit's interpretation. If we read it from our own understanding, we may find it's lacking the power that gives us Life.

Knowing this first, that no prophecy of Scripture is of any private interpretation, for prophecy never came by the will of man, but holy men of God spoke as they were moved by the Holy Spirit. -2 Peter 1:20-21 NKJV

We should invite the Spirit to discern what we are reading. Christ said, "I will ask the Father, and he will give you another advocate to help you and be with you forever—the Spirit of truth."[77] So often, we read scripture because we were told we should read it every day. We read the Word of God to become the Word of God. *"For the Word of God is alive and active. Sharper than any double-edged sword, it penetrates even to dividing soul and spirit, joints and marrow; it judges the thoughts and attitudes of the heart."*[78] At times, we may read it like we are reading any other book, usually quickly hoping to glean some inspiration for the day. Then there are times when we want to take a deep dive into the scriptures. Although studying the scriptures by yourself is helpful, studying with a group will give you the advantage of other people's understanding and wisdom as well.

So how do we read the Word of God to renew our mind? Often when we think of the word meditation as it relates to the Bible, we think of David, a young shepherd boy and the King of Israel. Scripture tells us David spent a great deal of time meditating on God and His word, *"Oh how I love your law! It is my meditation all the day.*[79]*"* and *"I will ponder all your work, and meditate on your mighty deeds."*[80] David understood its importance and power to mold him into the man God would use in a mighty way. It also shows us a humble David who relied on God to show him the best way to live his life. He affectionately referred to himself as the apple of God's eye.[81]

I would like to suggest another way to read scripture that enables the words to become more personal. First, pray for the guidance of the Holy Spirit to select the scripture you will read, and ask for discernment on the meaning it has for you. When you read the passage of scripture, usually a paragraph in length, read it slowly and intentionally from your heart. After you are done, take a minute to reflect on whether any word or a phrase stood out for you. Continue to read it two more times the same way. I find God reveals a depth in the scriptures not seen when we hurry through them. This is to open yourself up to hear from God through the scriptures. It exposes us to the truth, and it will renew our mind.

What would our life look like if we lived our daily experiences from a place of truth? Is it realistic to think we can always be truthful towards others and ourselves? I confess, I have lied to people and even to those I love. I don't like saying that out loud, but there it is. I would suspect you have done the same. Why is it difficult sometimes to tell the truth? For me, at times it was easier to lie than to possibly hurt someone's feelings. It also helped to avoid a possible confrontation. Although I believed my intentions were good—it was still a lie. It wasn't until I read scripture about God's feelings on the subject that I realized it was harming me to do so. I am only going to share one verse, but I encourage you to study the Bible and see what it says about lying. "Lying lips are an abomination to the Lord, but those who deal truthfully are His delight."[82] It makes sense that He would not want us to mislead or deceive one another. Love directs us to be truthful.

Another way we can renew our mind is to avoid the lies we tell ourselves and stop spending time evaluating situations unfavorably and not truthfully. If we really began to evaluate the truthfulness of our thoughts, we would find there is plenty of opportunity to interject truth. For instance, I may think, "Why am I writing this book, no one is going to read it anyway." The truth is someone is going to read it, even if only family and friends. So, with a little self-talk, I will make a statement back to myself and say, "People will read this book." I consider this practice my Truth Replacement Therapy. As I go through my day, if my mind pushes out a thought that is not true, I say so, "That's not true," and then say what is true. It's important that we are feeding ourselves truth. As we know, we are what we eat! It is a tremendous help if we stay focused on truth: *whatever is true, whatever is honorable, whatever is just, whatever is pure, whatever is lovely, whatever is commendable, if there is any excellence, if there is anything worthy of praise, think about these things.*[83] When we follow this amazing advice our consciousness levels increase, allowing for a more favorable life perspective. And more importantly, we will be more like Christ.

When we approach life from a place of truth, our mind will begin to be renewed and we begin to understand people and circumstances better. When we can come from a place of understanding, we become better advocates for Truth. Another way to say this is, when we can come from a place of love, others are more likely to hear the truth.

As we build our capacity for truth, we will possess a Godly wisdom. Who doesn't want to be wise? His truth will move us out of darkness into His marvelous light.

Therefore, *"Let the word of Christ dwell in you richly, teaching and admonishing one another in all wisdom, singing psalms and hymns and spiritual songs, with thankfulness in your hearts to God."[84]*

Chapter 7

The Practice of Love

"You shall love the Lord your God with all your heart, with all your soul, and with all your mind. This is the first and great commandment. And the second is like it: You shall love your neighbor as yourself."[85]

It may sound strange to have to practice love. You may feel it doesn't require practice; love just is, or it just happens to us. There is so much more to love than we might think! It has depth to it, and love expands as we go deeper into its richness. I am convinced our primary purpose in life is to learn what love truly is and how to live it out responsibly in our daily lives. We have learned most of what we know about love from the people in our lives, music, books, movies, TV, and social media. So much of what we have learned, quite frankly, isn't love at all. I believe the Holy Spirit wants to teach us how to truly love. To truly love means to respect and honor others, and to give love the way we want to receive love—unconditionally.

Love is a powerful emotion, but more importantly, it is a state of being. This state of being is the soil from which we become open to greater possibilities of who we truly are. Love can provide the freedom needed to open a window to begin to see life from a fuller perspective. When love is experienced, it establishes the beauty of its intention, and the love will come alive within us. This love is immensely powerful and will transmit and expand itself towards others. The energy in love has the potential to open a portal to draw us closer to God and one another.

If we feel guilty or ashamed of loving someone, we experience pain and suffering. A guilty conscience keeps us separated from our help, the Spirit of God. When we accept the feelings of love, we can invite the Spirit to help us understand them, and what to do with them without compromising our values. The Spirit will transform our love into something beautiful.

The journey of love brings with it an opportunity to begin and end, with love being our sole purpose, while we have breath to experience it to its fullness. To place our feet on that pathway, however, is to place ourselves on an exhilarating ride. The journey will likely take us to places of deep sorrow and places of high ecstasy. Sorrow and ecstasy are two of the hallmarks of romantic love when experienced fully.

One of our most memorable life experiences is to love someone for the first time, someone other than our family, and know they love us too. Our hearts are awakened to this immense feeling of love, full of innocence and joy. It feels like we are on top of the world. It feels like we can fly! It is the most significant opening to what the expression of God's love feels like. On the flip side, we experience sorrow beyond our ability to feel comforted if the relationship ends. Thankfully, both the elation and the sadness are only temporary, and we bounce back to where love is more manageable.

Navigating our journey with love would be easier if we had discovered God's love initially, but most of us find love in others first. What a difference it would make in all our relationships to know how to love unconditionally, as God loves us—to love an imperfect person perfectly. We tend to build on our capacity to love based on lessons learned in all our relationships, whether romantic, family, friends, or other relationships. The journey can be rough and is not for the faint-hearted. But God uses our love relationships and lessons we learn from them, to mold us into His likeness. God is Love,[86] and since He dwells within us, we have the capacity to experience love fully. We need to evaluate our hearts to begin the process of removing anything that is not love, so we can increase our capacity for it.

Life gives us many reasons to withdraw our love. With love comes vulnerability, and the fear of getting hurt. However, it's the price we may have to pay when we open ourselves up to experience love. The one thing we all have in common is we don't love perfectly. We may start our love adventure in a fully engaging self-mode, where we want to be the focus of the relationship. We want all the attention, and we are primarily interested in others loving us. We see these types of relationships among teenagers and people in their twenties. As we mature, we expand our love to include others. We begin to recognize love as a two-way street. We become capable of loving others deeply from our heart. A person fully mature in love sees themselves as love and extends it freely. They see Christ in others and there is a reverence and respect in the relationship.

Love begins with a focus from our physical being, then moves deeper for a more thoughtful and heartful experience, and finally to a more soulful love. As we are maturing, we will notice there is a wooing from the Holy Spirit to make some corrections in relationships that don't honor love. We will find He wants our relationships to align with these characteristics:

> *"Love is patient, love is kind. It does not envy, it does not boast, it is not proud. It does not dishonor others, it is not self-seeking, it is not easily angered, it keeps no record of wrongs. Love does not delight in evil but rejoices with the truth. It always protects, always trusts, always hopes, always perseveres."* [87]

I've found one of the primary benefits of practicing Christian meditation is how it softens our heart and brings forward love we haven't experienced before. It feels like love supersized! The love moves from a transient feeling to a state of being. Love becomes the basis for how I am engaging with life and am interacting with others. This new love masterfully integrates into our personality. It provides clarity and understanding in our conversations. We lose the desire to become divisive. Instead, we look for ways to unite.

Love will encourage us to make corrections in our lives. The biggest obstacle to making these changes is our inability to conquer fear. Where there is fear, love cannot be perfected.[88] When the errors are addressed, more love pours in. Fortunately, there are practices to assist in making love our primary purpose.

FORGIVENESS

Since God has demonstrated how to love better than anyone else, it seems wise to consider His instruction and example of love. The most important aspect of His love is His forgiveness. "God demonstrates his love for us in that while we were still sinners, Christ died for us."[89] This most holy act provided reconciliation to those who believe Jesus died to take away our sins. Thus, Jesus removed our shame and guilt, allowing us to start a new life in Him. How eloquently Paul shares this blessing with us.

For God was pleased to have all his fullness dwell in him (Christ), and through him to reconcile to himself all things, whether things on earth or things in heaven, by making peace through his blood, shed on the cross. Once you were alienated from God and were enemies in your minds because of your evil behavior. But now he has reconciled you by Christ's physical body through death to present you holy in his sight, without blemish and free from accusation.[90]

It is a pure, unconditional love providing such complete provision for our salvation, one that makes us whole and innocent now! Even if our mind can't conceive it, it is true. We can embrace His love and His acceptance just as we are—flaws and all. And if we can believe this for ourselves, we can also believe it for everyone.

His love invites us to forgive ourselves and others. Forgiveness isn't easy, but it is essential to experiencing the fullness of Christ. How can we expand in love, if we are holding fear, anger, and disappointment in our hearts? The answer is we can't. These negative emotions are contrary to love, and they need to go. They not only affect us emotionally and spiritually, but these harmful emotions also affect us physically. Karen Swarts, a director at John Hopkins Hospital writes,

> "There is an enormous physical burden to being hurt and disappointed." Chronic anger puts you into a fight-or-flight mode, which results in numerous changes in heart rate, blood pressure and immune response. Those changes, then, increase the risk of depression, heart disease and diabetes, among other conditions. Forgiveness, however, calms stress levels, leading to improved health."

Why should I forgive? We forgive because we have been forgiven by God through Jesus Christ. We have received mercy and been released from the burden of sin. We are asked to extend it to others. There are some compelling scriptures exhorting us to do so.

❖ *"Therefore, if you are offering your gift at the altar and there remember that your brother or sister has something against you, leave your gift there in front of the altar. First go and be reconciled to them; then come and offer your gift.[91]*

❖ *Forgive, and you will be forgiven.[92]*

❖ *Be kind and compassionate to one another, forgiving each other, just as in Christ God forgave you.[93]*

❖ *Forgive us our trespasses as we forgive those who trespass against us.[94]*

Jesus said, Father, forgive them, for they do not know what they are doing. -Luke 23:34

We may feel by withholding forgiveness, we are hurting those who have hurt us. The truth is we are only harming ourselves. It is time to let it go and allow love to take its rightful place in our heart.

When and how should I forgive? We should forgive anytime we feel negative emotions, such as hostility, unproductive anger that leads to malice and hatred, jealousy and so on. Because we too must believe *they do not know what they are doing.*[95] There's a very helpful forgiveness practice I have used to help me forgive others. Find a nice quiet place to sit in silence for a few minutes and then ask God to reveal to you who you need to forgive. I found names of people came up in my heart. So, I had to let go of the hurt they inflicted on me, and I forgave them. This was not easy to do. But I felt an emotional release afterwards and allowed myself to have a good cry.

Then there are those we need to ask for forgiveness. We may have hurt someone and never addressed their pain. We can't even imagine the healing that comes from asking someone to forgive us. I had an experience with someone who had been deeply hurt and betrayed by their spouse. I watched and prayed for her during this difficult time. Years later I went to see her, and I asked how she was doing since the problem in her marriage. We talked about how things have changed for the better, but then she broke down crying saying, "He never said he was sorry." How heartbreaking it was for her to continue in the marriage without the benefit of an apology. How much healing could be realized over just two words, "I'm sorry." It has been said, "Love is never having to say you're sorry."[96] I disagree. An apology has tremendous healing power and should be used whenever appropriate.

What are some of the barriers to forgiveness? We have been hurt and others have hurt us. Most of us have been on both sides of this equation. We either need to forgive or we are owed an apology. Addressing forgiveness can be difficult. There may be some family or peer pressure to refrain from making amends, or you may not have been aware of the importance of getting our heart right. You may be thinking, "How wrong can it be—everyone holds a grudge?" Mostly people may think about it and be convicted to set the record straight but struggled to do it. As I said earlier, "Forgiveness is hard," but in light of God's love, so is holding on to negative emotions.

How do we open our hearts to forgive? We struggle sometimes to give and receive forgiveness because our egos want to withdraw love from the other person. We might say, "They need to pay for what they have done to me", or "They don't deserve my forgiveness." I have found picking the right attitude can start the process. For example, a healthy way to look at the situation could be, it is not what happened to me that matters as much as what I do with what happened. How can I turn the situation around for God's glory? We could invite God to help. I have found this is where the Holy Spirit does amazing work. We can seek to understand, instead of judging the other person. Matthew reminds us, "You hypocrite, first take the log out of your own eye, and then you will see clearly to take the speck out of your brother's eye.[97] We can show compassion. A Scripture passage that always stirs my heart is, "Above all, love each other deeply, because love covers a multitude of sins."[98] When all other strategies fail, let love find the way to heal the broken heart.

The forgiveness journey can take a lot of twists and turns. I have found I can't be too overly concerned about what may happen to others when I ask for forgiveness. I need to take responsibility for my side of the street. I need to take care of my own soul and not worry about what others are thinking or doing. Ultimately, I must decide what is more important--the pain and suffering I am experiencing, or the peace God offers me when I let it go and forgive. What they do is their own business.

Forgiving someone doesn't mean you go back into an unhealthy relationship. No one wins if that happens. If someone is not actively trying to get help, they are not likely to change. You may need to minimize or eliminate your exposure to them.

Forgiveness can have layers. For difficult situations, you may forgive someone to find out later that you still have resentment or anger towards them. Continue to work through the layers until the negative emotions are gone.

Perpetual forgiveness is harder to do, but with practice it becomes easier. It is letting go of the wrong when it happens. You extend grace to the other person the same way God does for you. This doesn't mean we don't address negative behavior; it means we don't let it take away our peace. Deal with the behavior, but don't hold onto the grievance. This is how we keep our soul clean and our relationship with God open.

Reconciliation goes beyond forgiveness and invites us to move full circle in the relationship. If enough healing has taken place, it can go back to how it was originally intended. I have experienced this in several of my relationships. It is amazing how God will work in the most difficult situations to bring the relationship to a beautiful place.

Sometimes the hardest person to forgive is ourselves. The truth is if we could forgive ourselves, we wouldn't need Jesus. He knows what you did and is just waiting for you to bring it to Him so He can free you from it. It is as simple as that, but so many of us hold on to our guilt and shame. We may feel as if we have done something unforgiveable. Well, we haven't. The truth is Christ already dealt with it. God has forgiven us for it. Now it is up to you to let the situation go. Once you let it go, there is no more conflict between you and God. There is only peace opening the way for love to flow in.

JUDGING OTHERS

It can be said that when I judge another person, I am revealing an unhealed part of myself. If I am seen by God as whole and innocent, then I need to first believe that about myself and then believe it for others. So if I am judging someone, it is likely it is something I am judging against myself. Have you ever made a judgement about someone else and then shortly afterwards you find yourself in the same or similar situation? The Word of God has made it clear *there is now no condemnation for those who are in Christ Jesus*[99]. Christ's vision is peace within us, others, and most importantly with God. We maintain our peace when we see others through a filter of love. No one has ever seen God; if we love one another, God abides in us and his love is perfected in us.[100] It is a beautiful life when we can freely and lovingly see others and not judge them. The Golden Rule, "Do to others as you want them to do to you,"[101] carries so much wisdom. I often think about how each one of us wants unconditional love and acceptance for who we are and yet we're so reluctant to give it to others—even to those we say we love.

A revered, wise man once asked his disciples, "How can we know when the darkness is leaving and the dawn is coming?"

"When can we see a tree in the distance and know that it is an elm and not a juniper," ventured one student.

"When we can see an animal and know that it is a fox and not a wolf," chimed in another.

"No," he said the old man, "Those things will not help us."

Puzzled, the student demanded, "How then can we know?"

The wise man drew himself up to his full stature and replied quietly, "We know the darkness is leaving and dawn is coming when we can see another person and know that this is our brother or our sister; otherwise, no matter what time it is--it is still dark."

There is nothing more important than getting our hearts right with God. For when we do, we open our capacity to love in ways we never thought possible. I am fully convinced; all our life experiences are for us to glean one thing--love truly is the answer, always! Knowing this has helped me understand why I am going through different situations in my life. It is a tremendous help getting me to the answer of the "whys" of life. As I navigate each one, I find my capacity to love has expanded. As love grows, so does the depth of my love for God. And with each passing day, He continues to draw me closer and closer to Himself.

EPILOGUE

Come close to God and God will come close to you.[102]

We have taken a journey through the practices within Christian meditation. We have learned how surrender, presence, stillness, prayer, renewing our mind and love are all essential in drawing us closer to God. It is no wonder the practice of Christian meditation accelerates our journey to wholeness. We are dismantling the ego at the same time that we are strengthening our spirit. We are tearing down old patterns of living and creating a new Life.

It is within this practice of Christian meditation that we explore many of the dimensions of the Kingdom of God. These practices are reminders that we are not separate from God. For separation drives us to manage and create relative to our own desires. The one common denominator in the type of work the self creates—always leads to fear. The road is riddled with anxiety. The one common denominator found in creating for the Kingdom of God is love and the path is established through peace. A perfect peace is promised to those whose mind stays on God because we trust in Him.[103]

Over time and with patience, the practices start to integrate perfectly into our persona. We will find it much easier to let things go by practicing surrender. By spending time in God's Presence, our presence will have a positive impact on our relationships. We will have a calming and peaceful demeanor from practicing stillness. We pray and renew our mind, so our lives become prayer and our actions are more aligned to the Word of God. We practice love to honor God's commandments and to be as God is. This is what you can look forward to if you just sit and receive from our Lord. Remember Jesus' promise, "Come to me, all you who are weary and burdened, and I will give you rest.[104]

My hope and prayer for you is that the Holy Spirit will encourage your heart to desire to spend time with the Holy Three--the Father, Son, and Holy Spirit. In a world full of noise and chaos, may we take time to drop beneath the thinking mind, to be present, unhindered by our ego, with love in our heart and with no agenda—just rest. Our willingness to surrender to this Rest will produce in us an unshakeable faith, one that will withstand anything the evil one throws our way. As Paul reminds us,

Finally, be strong in the Lord and in his mighty power. Put on the full armor of God, so that you can take your stand against the devil's schemes. For our struggle is not against flesh and blood, but against the rulers, against the authorities, against the powers of this dark world and against the spiritual forces of evil in the heavenly realms. Therefore put on the full armor of God, so that when the day of evil comes, you may be able to stand your ground, and after you have done everything, to stand. Stand firm then, with the belt of truth buckled around your waist, with the breastplate of righteousness in place, and with your feet fitted with the readiness that comes from the gospel of peace. In addition to all this, take up the shield of faith, with which you can extinguish all the flaming arrows of the evil one. Take the helmet of salvation and the sword of the Spirit, which is the word of God.

And pray in the Spirit on all occasions with all kinds of prayers and requests. With this in mind, be alert and always keep on praying for all the Lord's people.[105]

I have written this book to serve as a support for you. I know how difficult it can be to maintain the practice of Christian meditation. But with God's help and the support of others, I have maintained my meditation practice for over 20 years. No one continues in anything that hasn't been of great value to them. So, practice with confidence, knowing the truth that our Lord doesn't show favoritism.[106] What He has done for me, He will also do for you.

ACKNOWLEDGEMENTS

There is so much gratitude and love to everyone who had faith in my ability to write and publish this book. There are so many people who have supported the process to get this book published. All glory to God for the inspiration and guidance to write this book.

Special thanks to my husband, Bill Yerkes for his love and encouragement to follow as the Lord leads in my life. I am grateful for my family and friend's support—those amazing cheerleaders supporting me spiritually and emotionally.

There are those who were willing to review the book to make it flow better, checking for grammar and spelling errors, and asked me to say more about the content that was not clear. Those gifted and amazing people are George Allen, Leah Chrest, Jennifer Kurman, Odessa Patton, and Vicki Simek!

It was difficult for me to find the time write, so I reached out to Jo Nelsen, an amazing writing coach to keep me on task. Thank you for your encouragement and creative ideas!

NOTES

All scripture references are from the New International Version unless stated otherwise. All scripture was referenced from Biblegateway.com.

Prologue

[1] Luke 10:41-42
[2] Sinner's Prayer, found on page 32.
[3] John 8:36
[4] Thomas Keating, O.C.S.O. was an American Catholic monk and priest of the Order of Cistercians of the Strict Observance. Keating was known as one of the principal developers of Centering Prayer, a contemporary method of contemplative prayer that emerged from St. Joseph's Abbey, Spencer, Massachusetts. Wikipedia

Chapter 1

[5] Psalm 46:10
[6] From The Cloud of Unknowing with the Book of Privy Counsel; page 11.
[7] Philippians 1:6
[8] Hebrews 12:28-29 NRSV
[9] 1 Thessalonians 5:17 NRSV

Chapter 2

[10] Matthew 6:10
[11] Matt 17:20
[12] Jeremiah 29:10-14
[13] Acts 17:27
[14] James 4:8
[15] Luke 12:7
[16] Jeremiah 1:5
[17] Eph 3:18
[18] 2 Peter 3:9
[19] Col. 2:9-10
[20] John 8:12
[21] 2 Timothy 1:9
[22] Acts 14:3
[23] John 1:16
[24] Romans 5:20 &1 Cor 15:10
[25] Acts 15:11
[26] Romans 11:6
[27] Hebrews 4:16
[28] Hebrews 7:25
[29] Eph 2:8
[30] Thomas Merton in The New Man
[31] Romans 5:1-2
[32] Hebrews 10:22
[33] Eph 3:12
[34] Hebrews 11:1
[35] Romans 1:12
[36] Matthew 23-27
[37] 2 Corinthians 5:7
[38] Hebrews 12:2
[39] 2 Timothy 2:13
[40] Luke 17:5

[41] Galatians 5:22-23

Chapter 3

[42] Acts 17:28a
[43] Luke 17:21 KJV
[44] 1 Corinthians 3:16
[45] Matthew 28:20
[46] Col. 3:11 NIV
[47] Gal 5:13-18
[48] John 15:4

Chapter 4

[49] 2 Corinthians 5:17
[50] Phil 3:13 NASB
[51] John 16:33
[52] Isaiah 9:6
[53] John 14:27
[54] Psalm 46:10

Chapter 5

[55] Jeremiah 30:21
[56] 1 Corinthians 2:9
[57] Genesis 41:14-16
[58] Genesis 50:20
[59] Phil. 4:6
[60] Luke 5:15 & 16
[61] Matthew 6:9-13
[62] Mark 11:22-24
[63] James 5:14
[64] Romans 8:26 & 27

[65] James 5:16
[66] 1 Corinthians 14:1
[67] Matthew 6:9-13
[68] Revelation 3:20
[69] Psalm 38:15

Chapter 6

[70] Romans 12:2
[71] Psalm 32:8
[72] Matt. 6:10
[73] Philippians 2:13
[74] Col 2:9-10
[75] John 14:6
[76] 2 Timothy 3:13-17
[77] John 14:16
[78] Hebrews 4:12
[79] Psalm 119:97
[80] Psalm 77:12
[81] Psalm 17:8
[82] Proverbs 12:22 NKJV
[83] Philippians 4:8 ESV
[84] Col. 3:16 ESV

Chapter 7

[85] Matthew 22:37-39
[86] 1 John 4:8
[87] 1 Corinthians 13:4-7
[88] 1 John 4:18
[89] Romans 5:8
[90] Colossians 1:19-22
[91] Matthew 5:23-24

[92] Luke 6:37
[93] Ephesians 4:32
[94] Matthew 6:12
[95] Luke 23:34
[96] Love means never having to say you're sorry" is a catchphrase based on a line from the Erich Segal novel, Love Story and was popularized by its 1970 film adaptation starring Ali MacGraw and Ryan O'Neal. Wikipedia
[97] Matthew 7:5
[98] 1 Peter 4:8
[99] Romans 8:1
[100] 1 John 4:12
[101] Luke 6:31

Epilogue

[102] James 4:8
[103] Isaiah 26:3
[104] Matt 11:28
[105] Ephesians 6:10-18
[106] Romans 2:11

If you liked this book, consider one of these!

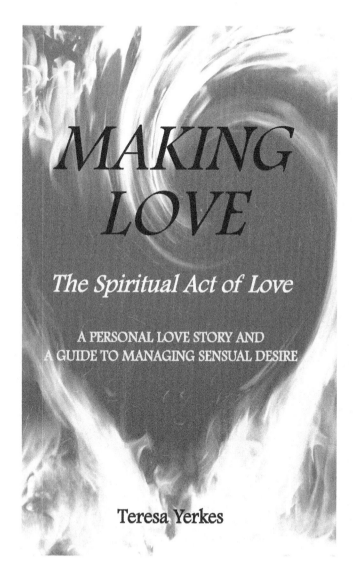

MAKING
LOVE

The Spiritual Act of Love

A PERSONAL LOVE STORY AND
A GUIDE TO MANAGING SENSUAL DESIRE

Teresa Yerkes

Made in the USA
Middletown, DE
24 June 2023